THIS WORKBOOK
BELONGS TO

____

CAPITAL LETTERS

A B C D

E F G H

I J K L

M N O P

CAPITAL LETTERS

Q R S T

U V W X

Y Z

small letters

a b c d

e f g h

i j k l

m n o p

small letters

q r s t

u v w x

y z

LEARNING LETTERS

Practice! Trace and then write the letter.

LEARNING LETTERS

Practice! Trace and then write the letter.

LEARNING LETTERS

Practice! Trace and then write the letter.

LEARNING LETTERS

Practice! Trace and then write the letter.

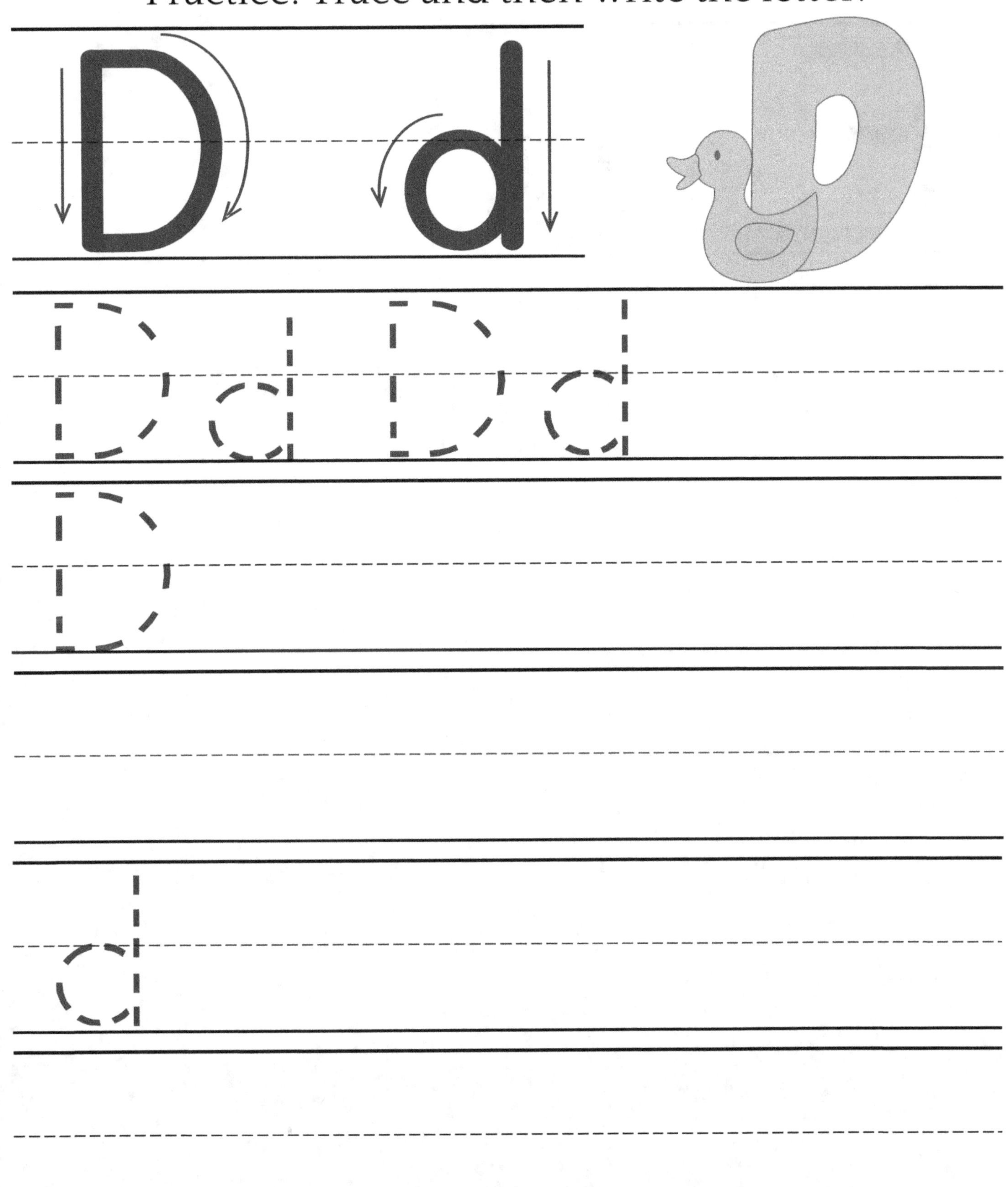

LEARNING LETTERS

Practice! Trace and then write the letter.

LEARNING LETTERS

Practice! Trace and then write the letter.

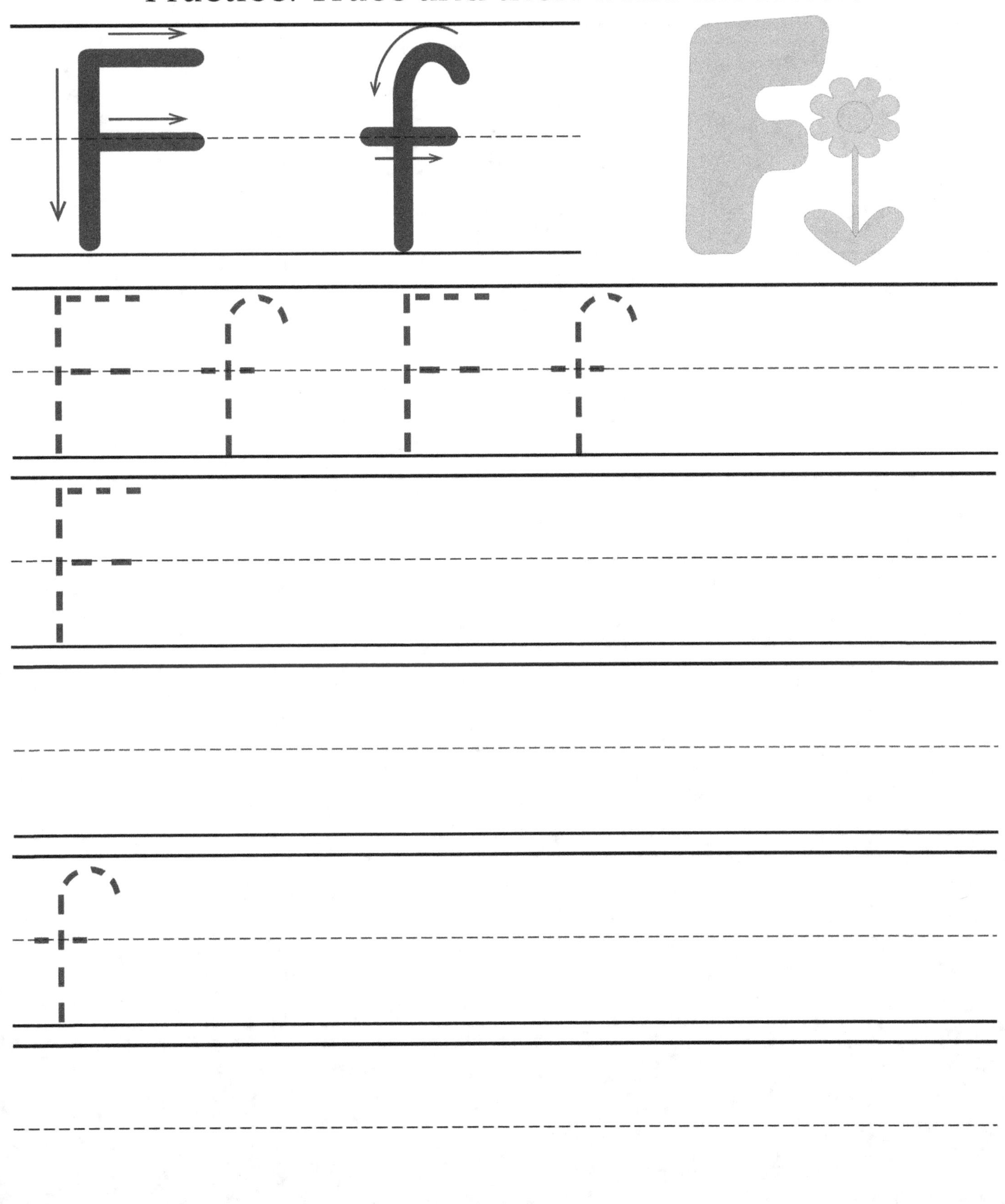

LEARNING LETTERS

Practice! Trace and then write the letter.

LEARNING LETTERS

Practice! Trace and then write the letter.

LEARNING LETTERS

Practice! Trace and then write the letter.

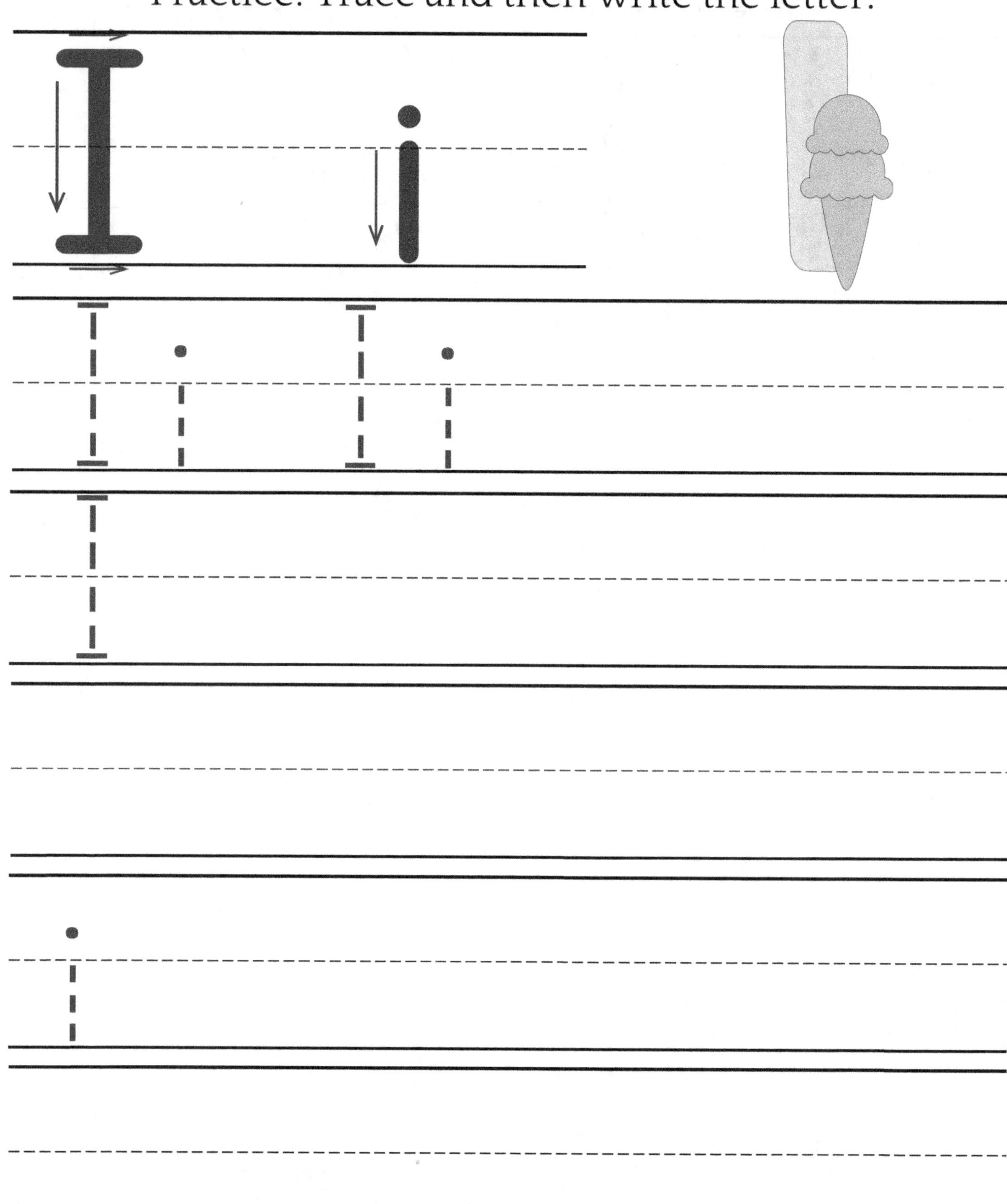

LEARNING LETTERS

Practice! Trace and then write the letter.

LEARNING LETTERS

Practice! Trace and then write the letter.

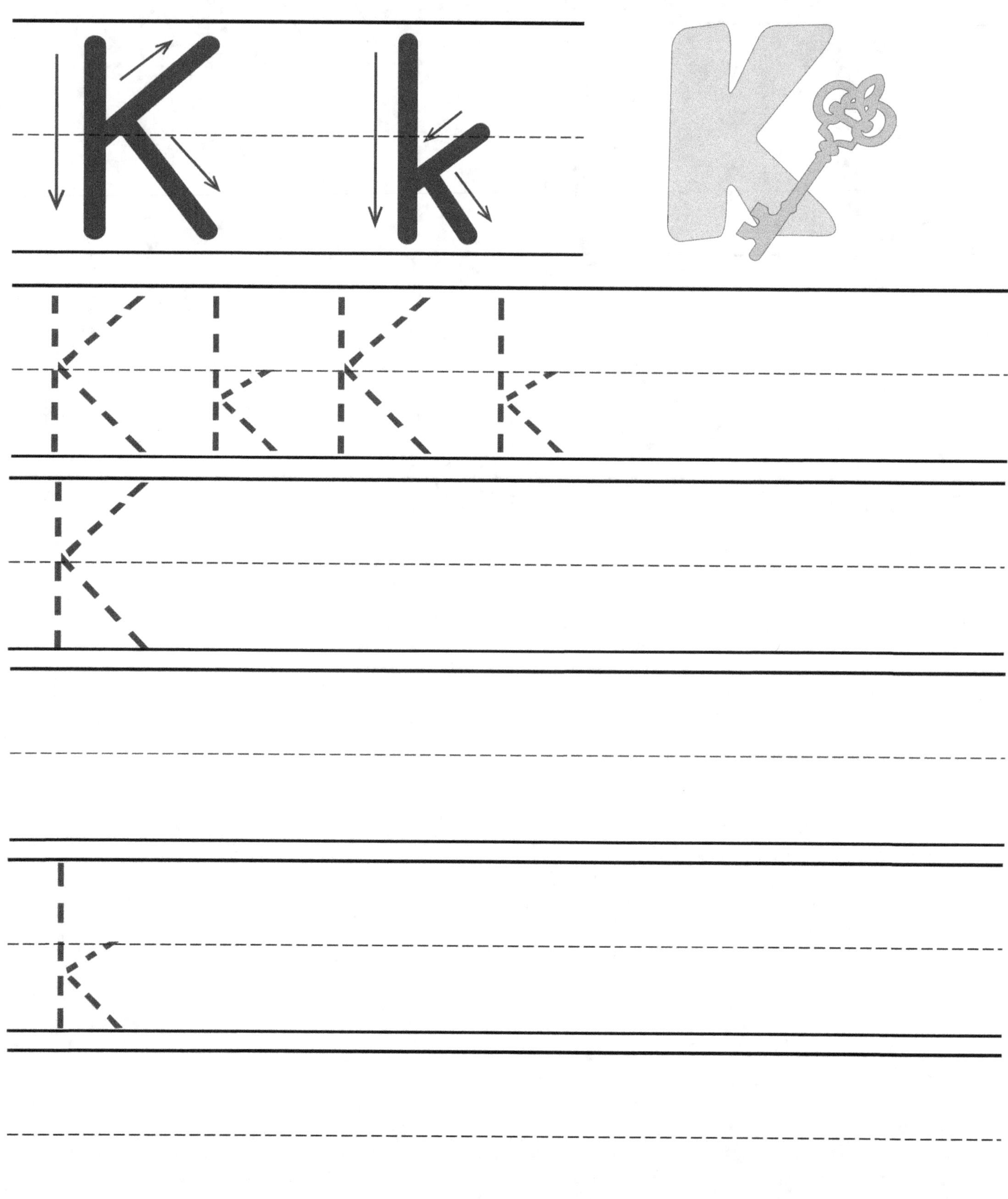

LEARNING LETTERS

Practice! Trace and then write the letter.

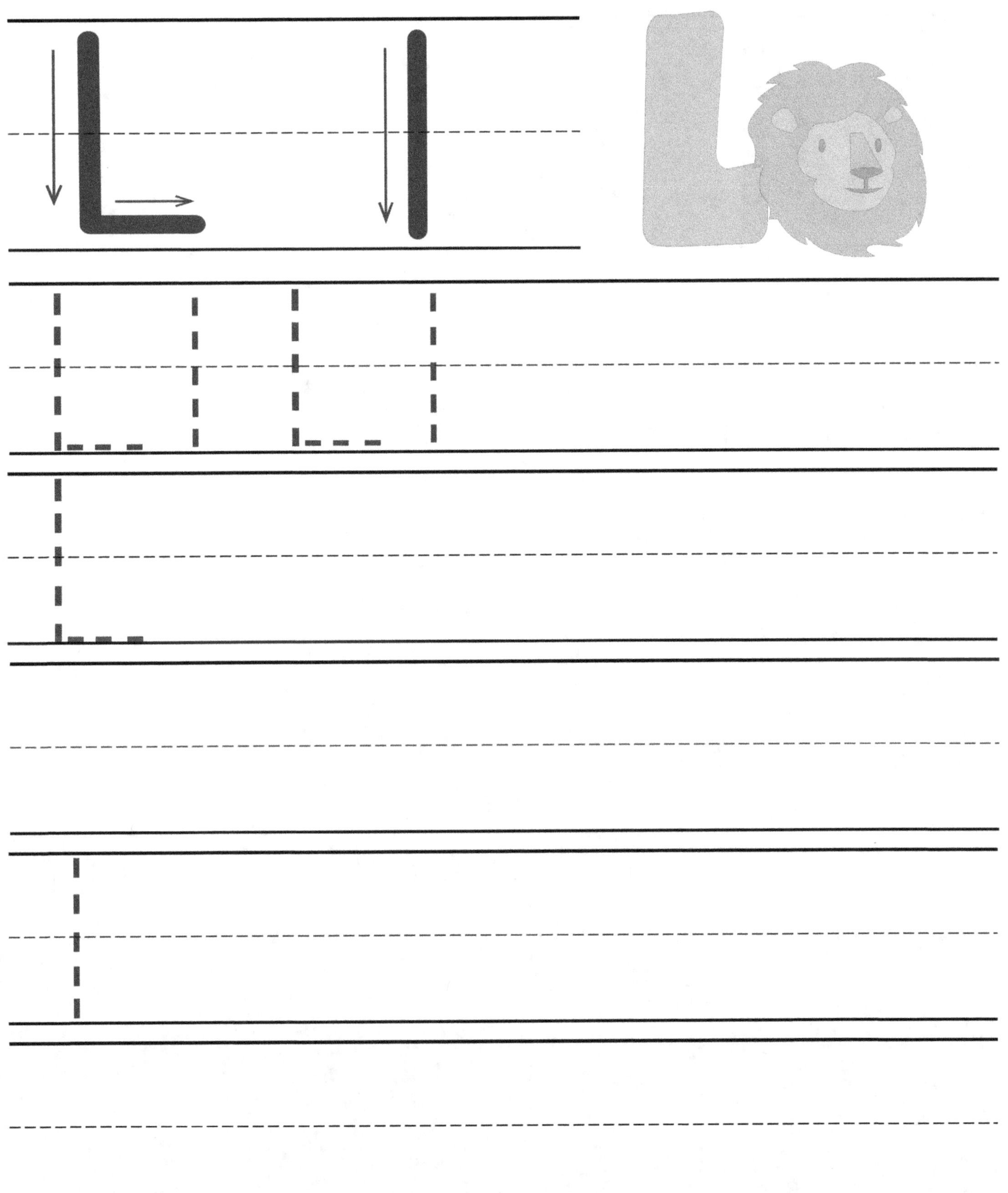

LEARNING LETTERS

Practice! Trace and then write the letter.

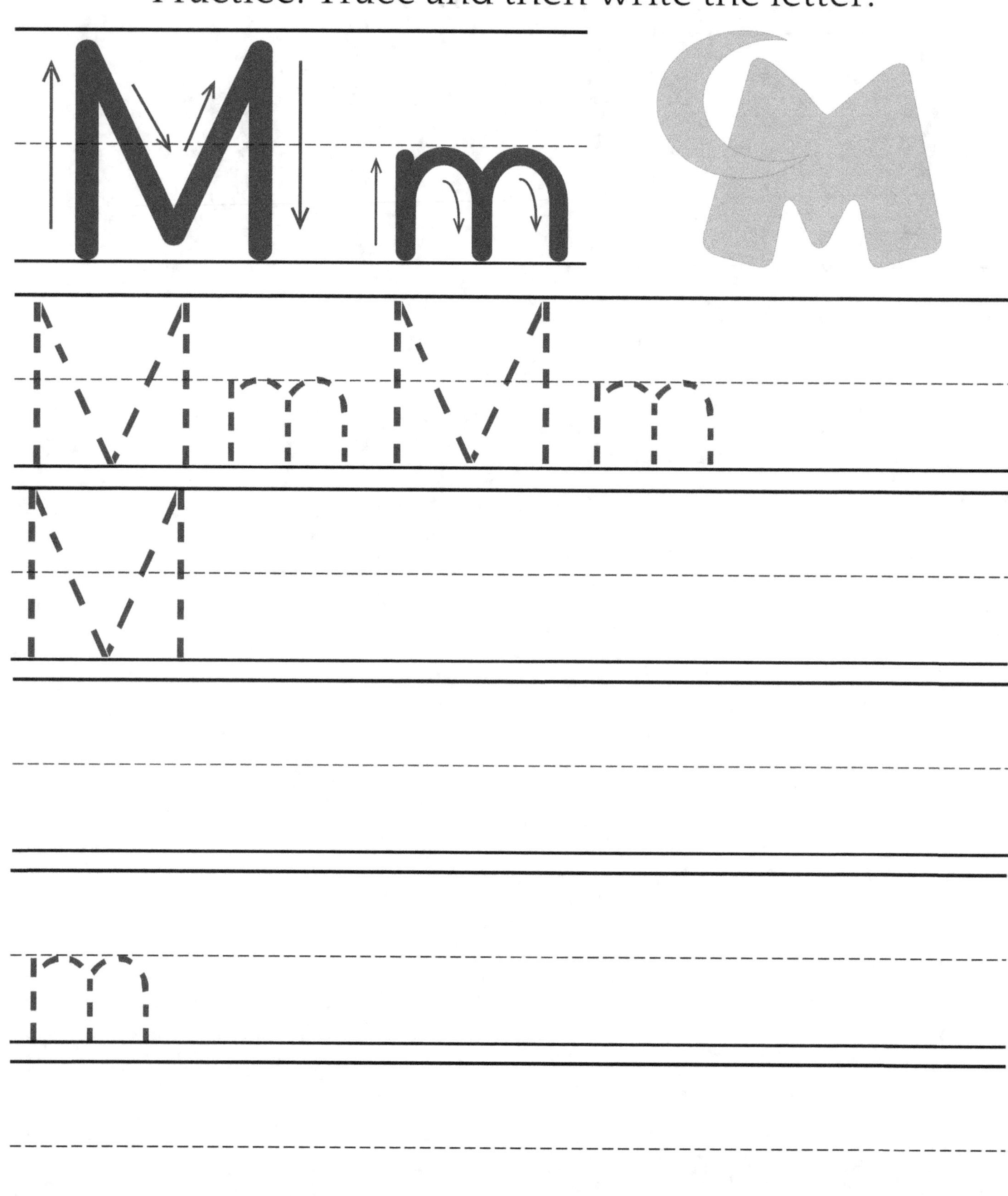

LEARNING LETTERS

Practice! Trace and then write the letter.

LEARNING LETTERS

Practice! Trace and then write the letter.

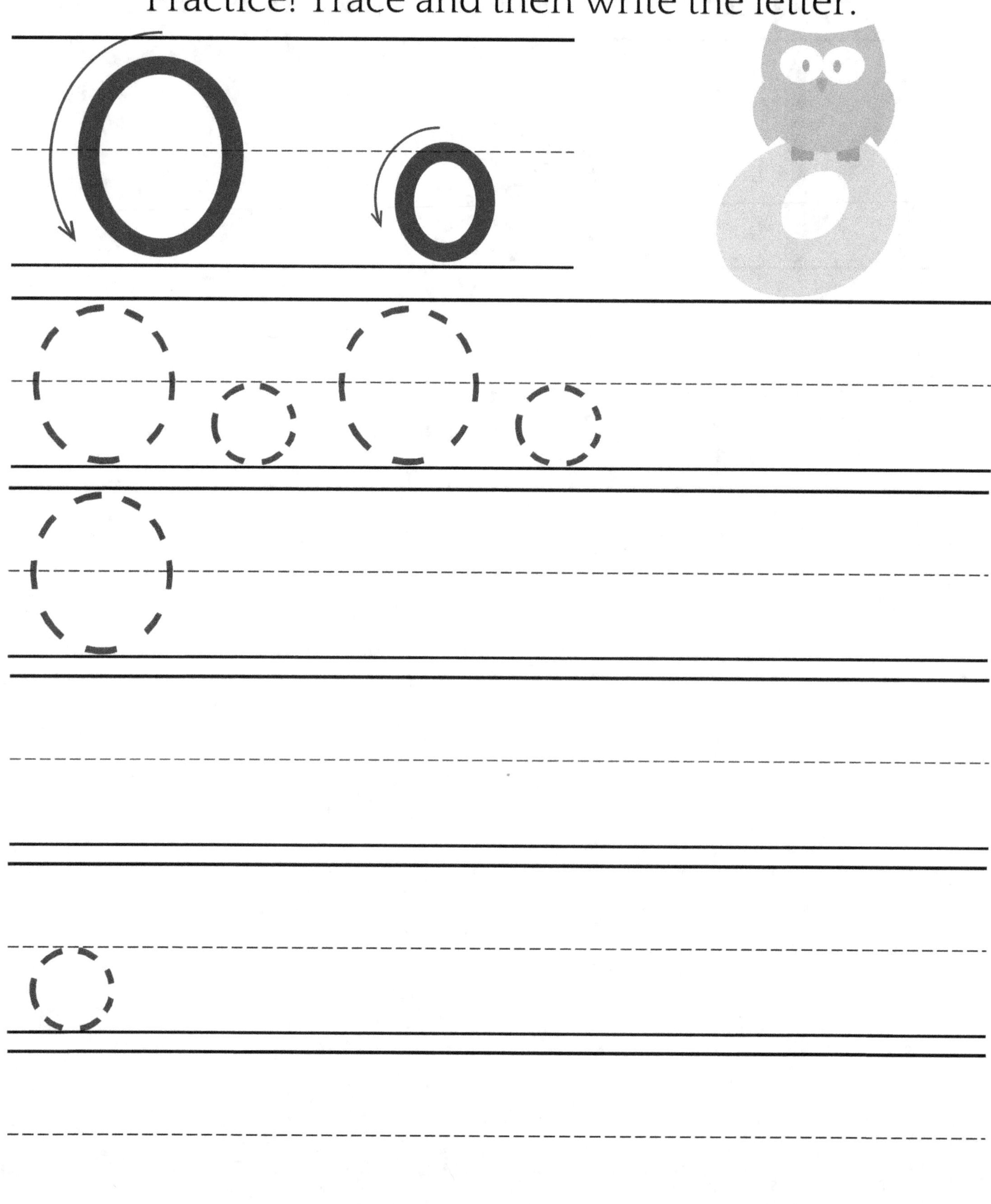

LEARNING LETTERS

Practice! Trace and then write the letter.

LEARNING LETTERS

Practice! Trace and then write the letter.

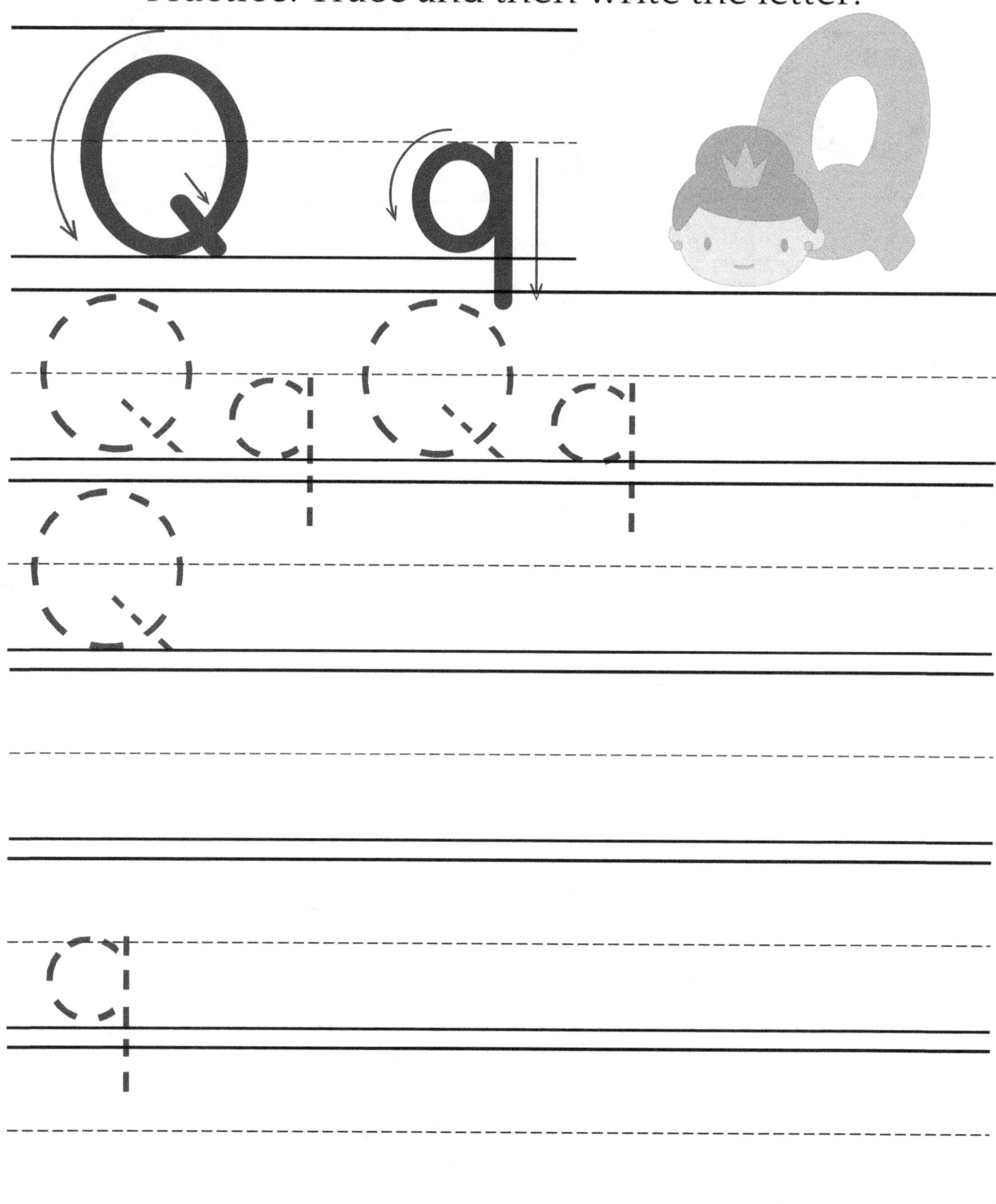

LEARNING LETTERS

Practice! Trace and then write the letter.

LEARNING LETTERS

Practice! Trace and then write the letter.

LEARNING LETTERS

Practice! Trace and then write the letter.

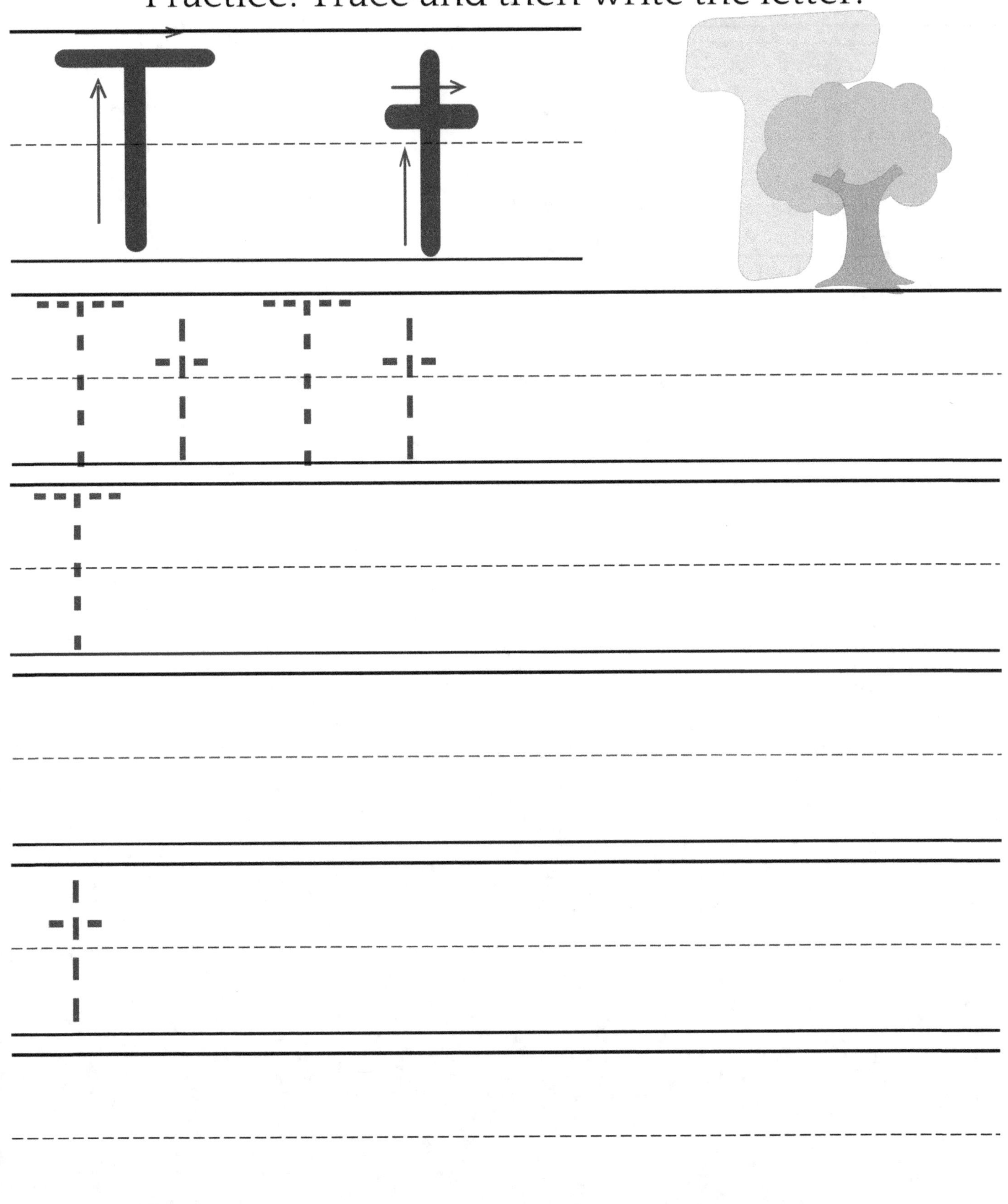

LEARNING LETTERS

Practice! Trace and then write the letter.

LEARNING LETTERS

Practice! Trace and then write the letter.

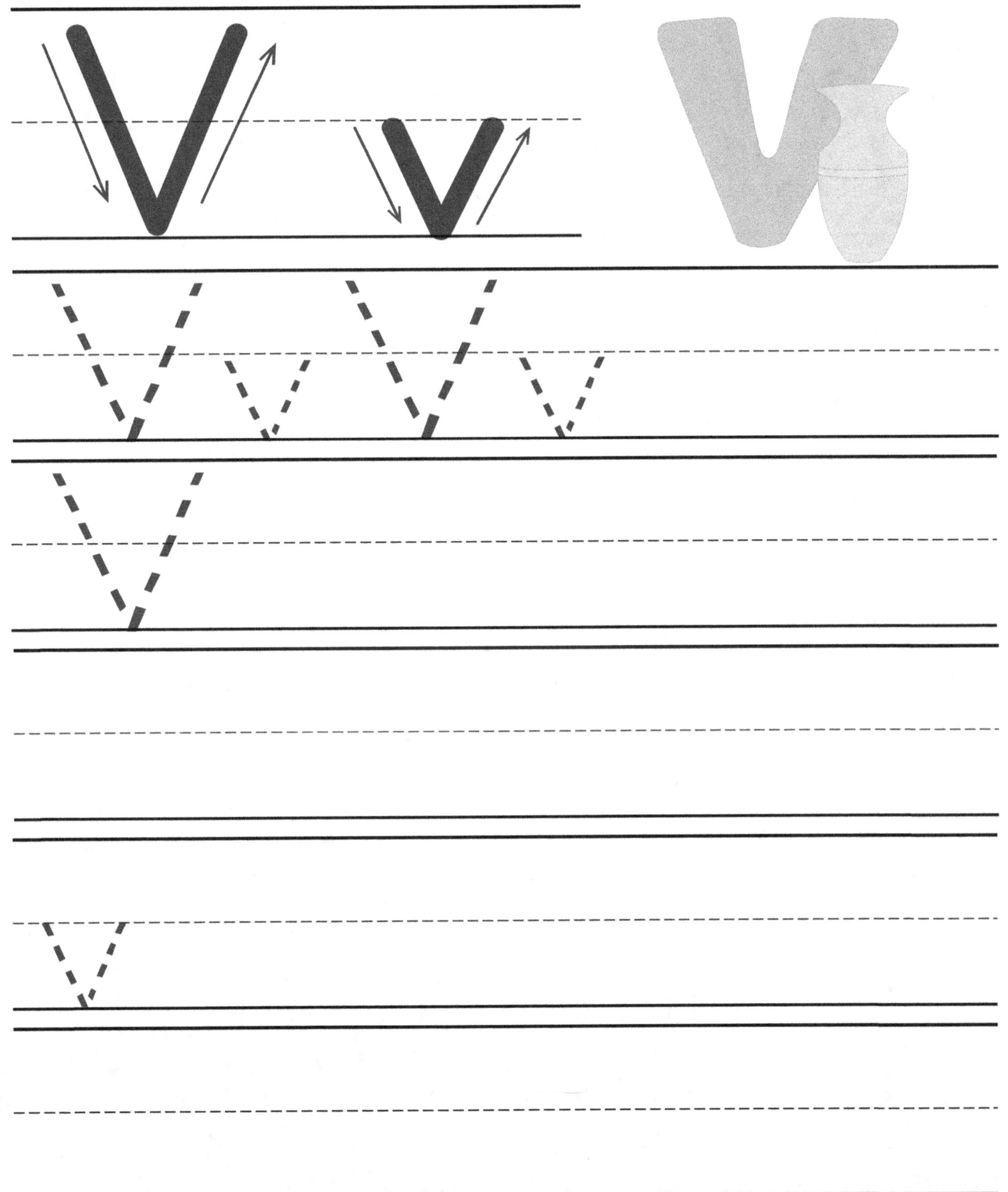

LEARNING LETTERS

Practice! Trace and then write the letter.

LEARNING LETTERS

Practice! Trace and then write the letter.

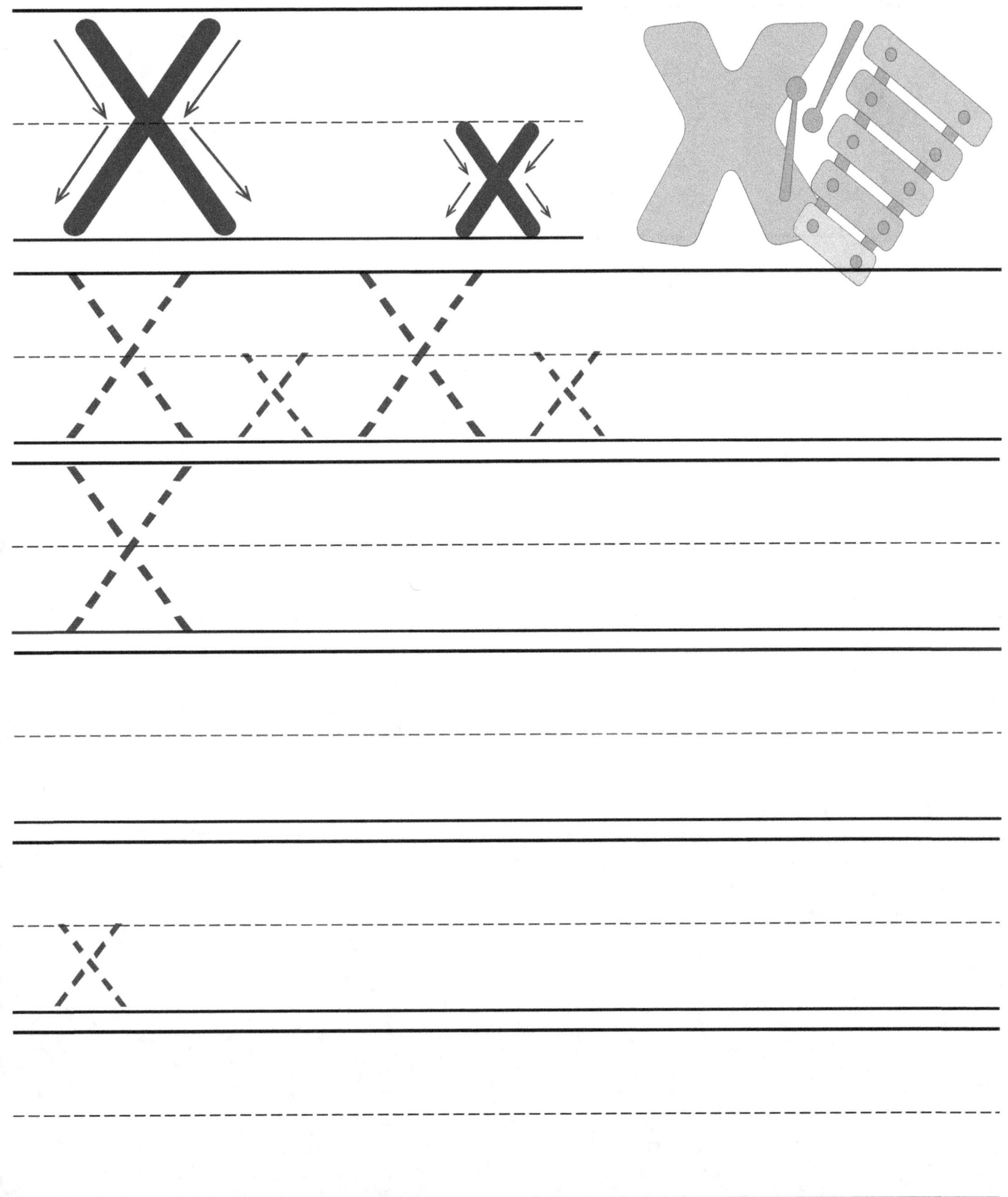

LEARNING LETTERS

Practice! Trace and then write the letter.

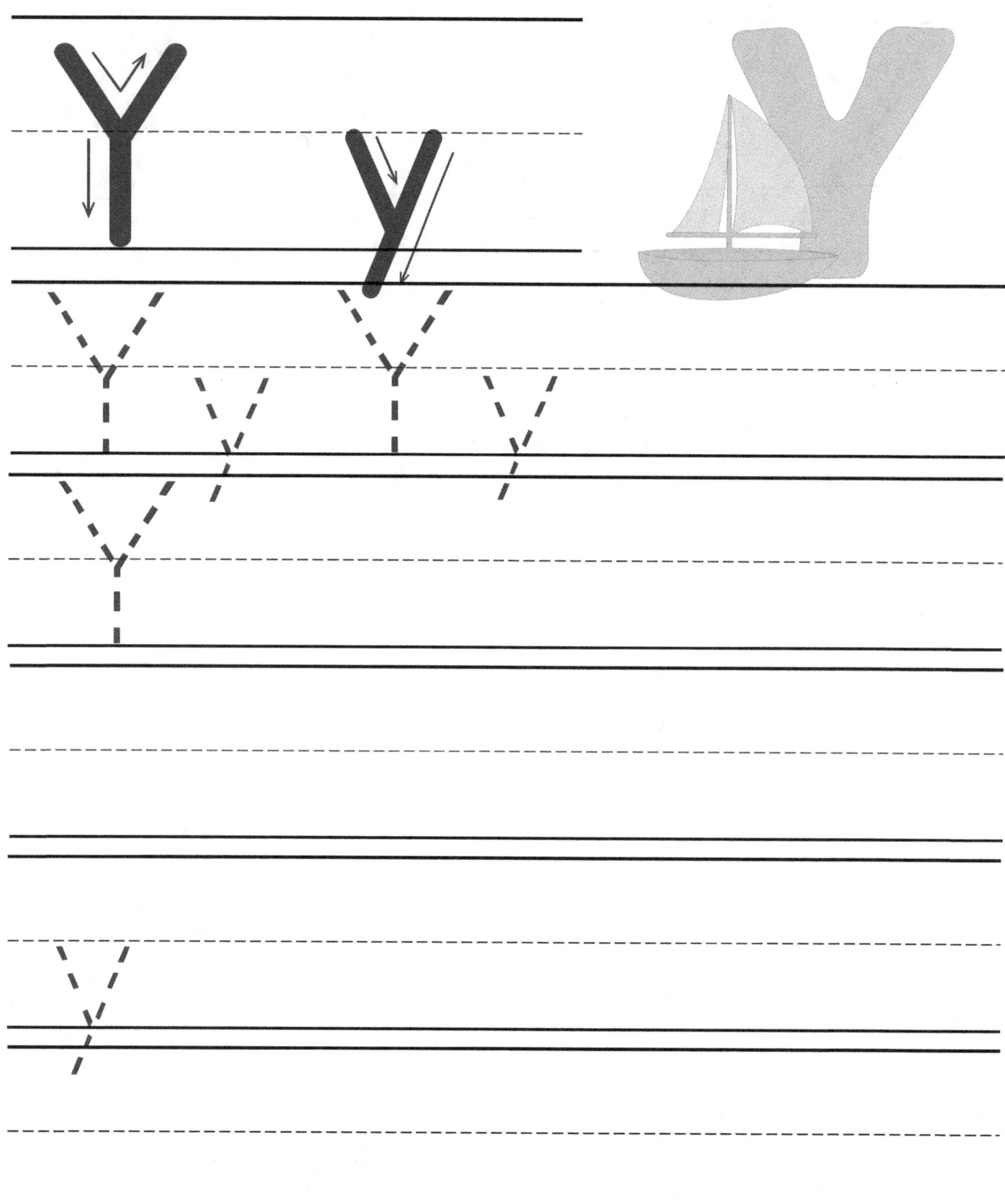

LEARNING LETTERS

Practice! Trace and then write the letter.

Practice Pages

Fill in the missing letter.

A B ☐ D

E ☐ G H

I J K ☐

M ☐ O P

Practice Pages

Fill in the missing letter.

Q R ☐ T

U V W ☐

Y ☐

Practice Pages

Fill in the missing letter.

a b c ___

e f ___ h

i ___ k l

___ n o p

Practice Pages

Fill in the missing letter.

ALPHABET

Trace the capital letters.

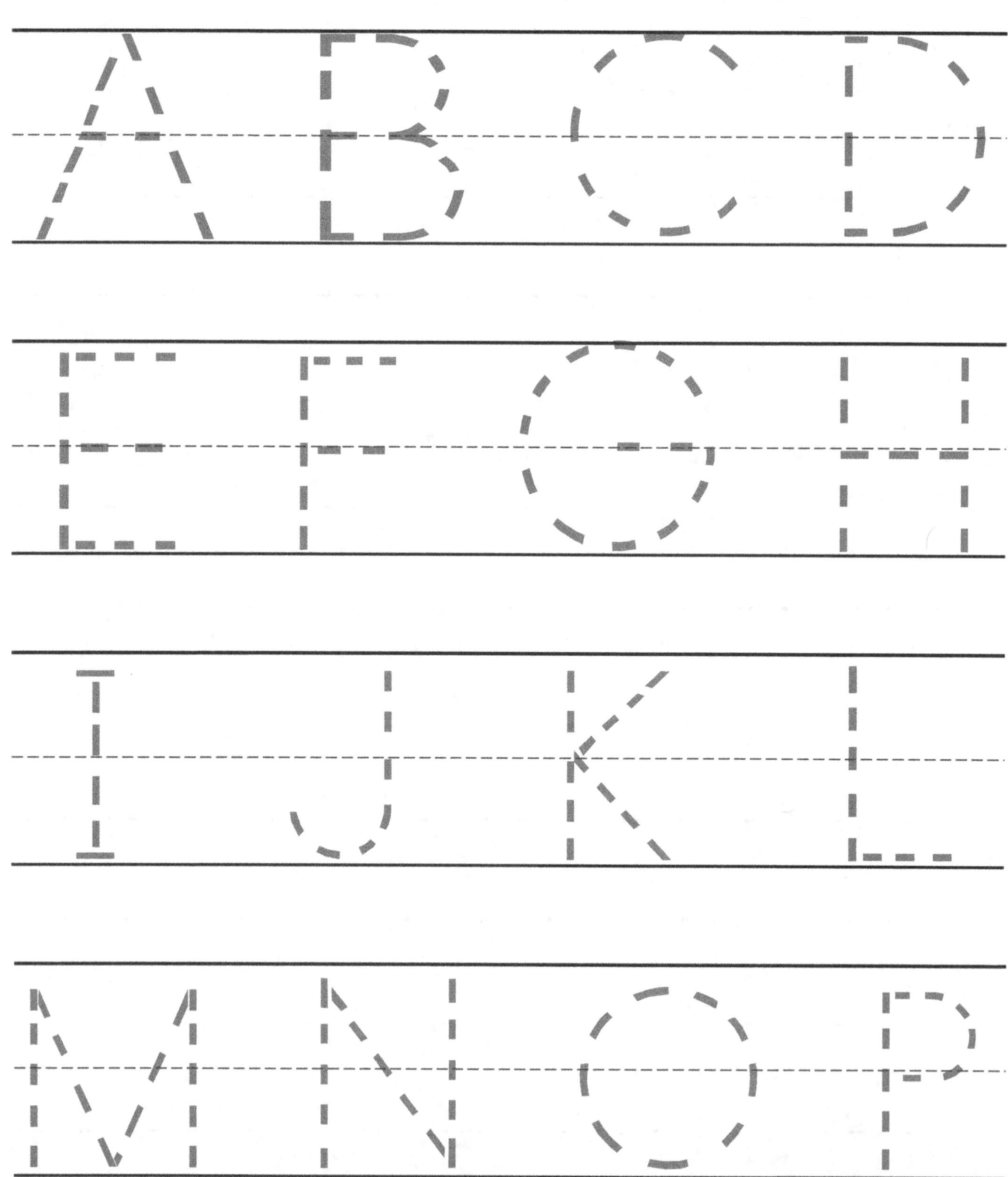

ALPHABET

Trace the capital letters.

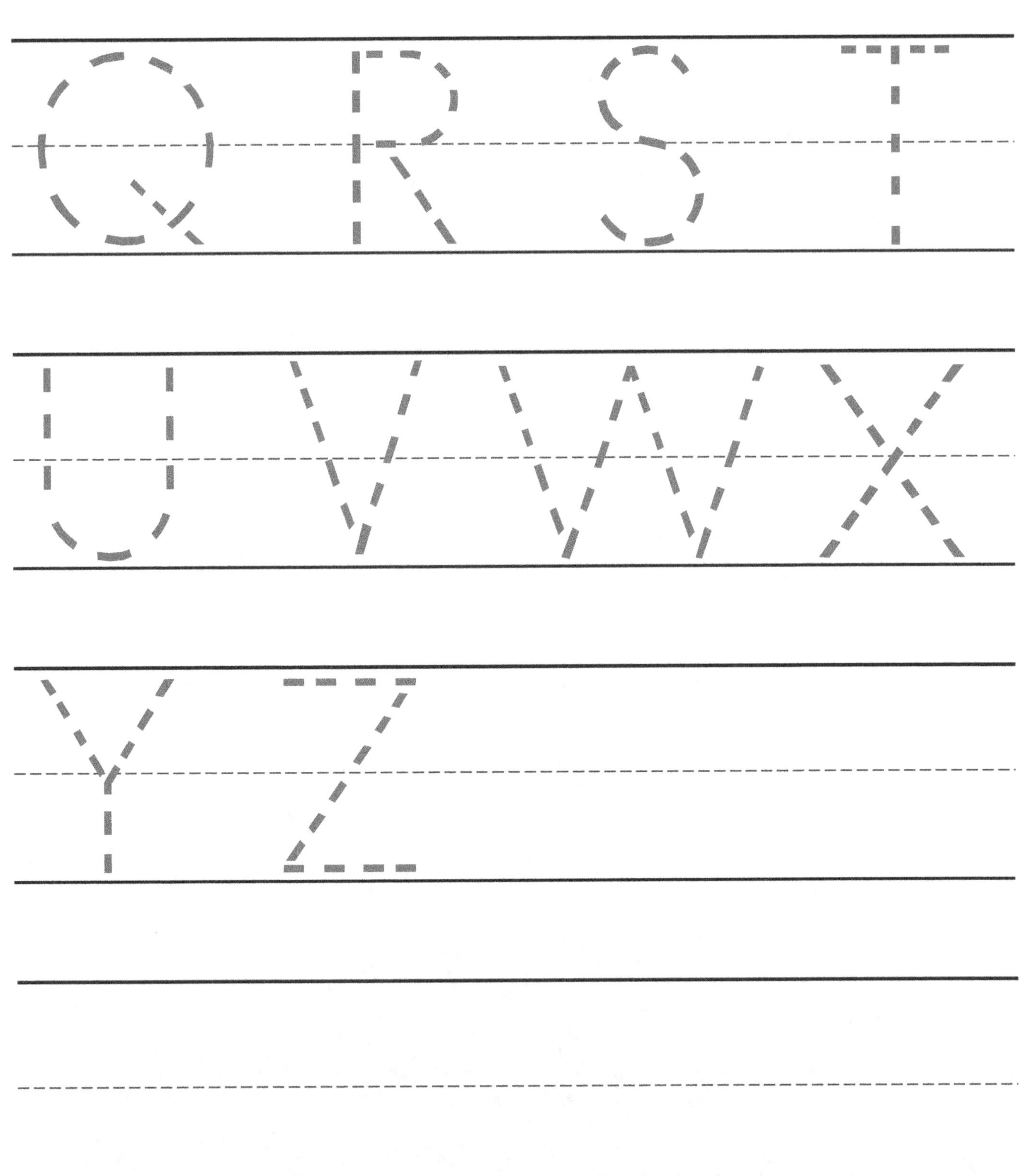

ALPHABET

Trace the capital letters.

ALPHABET

Trace the capital letters.

ALPHABET

Trace the small letters.

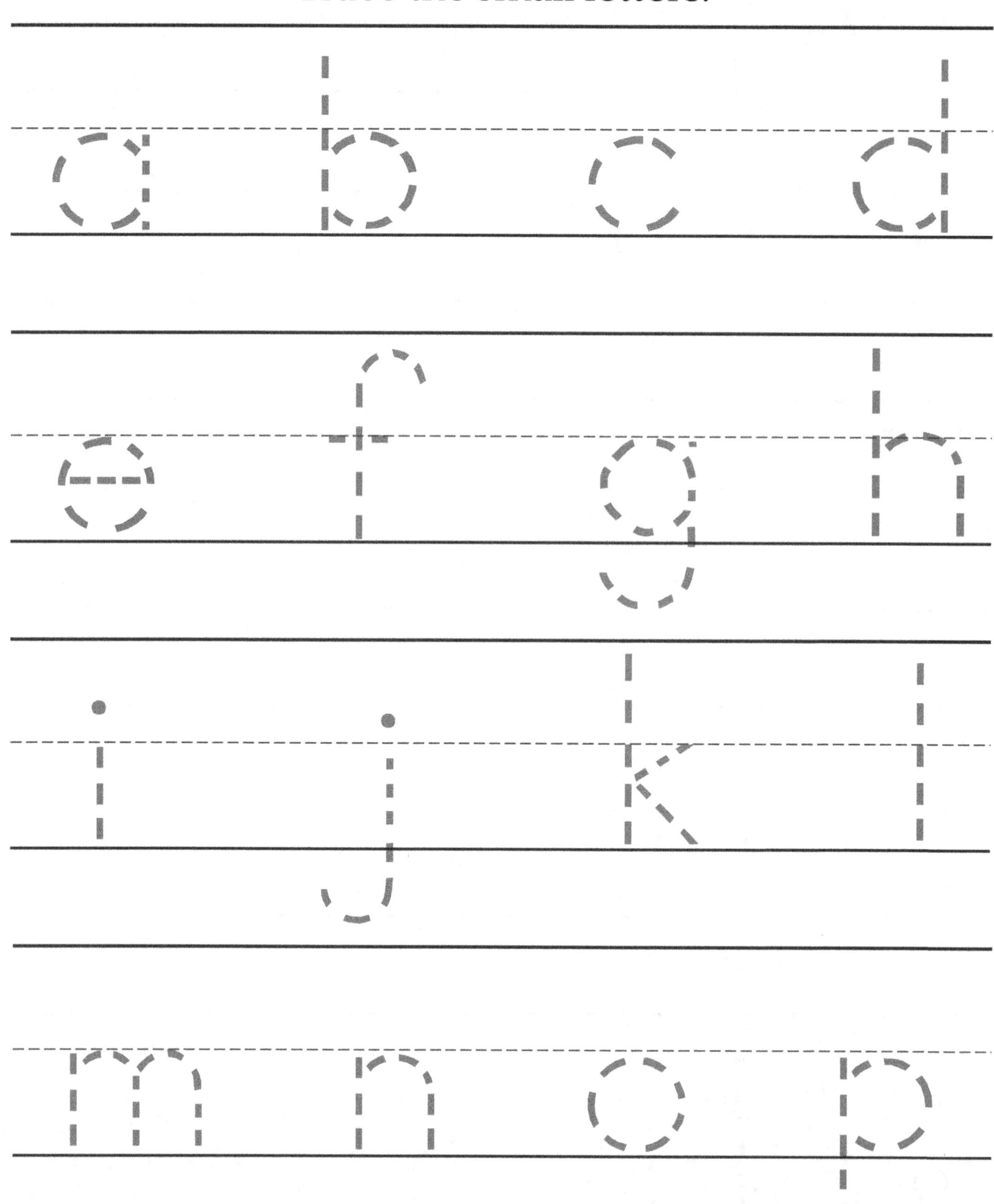

ALPHABET

Trace the small letters.

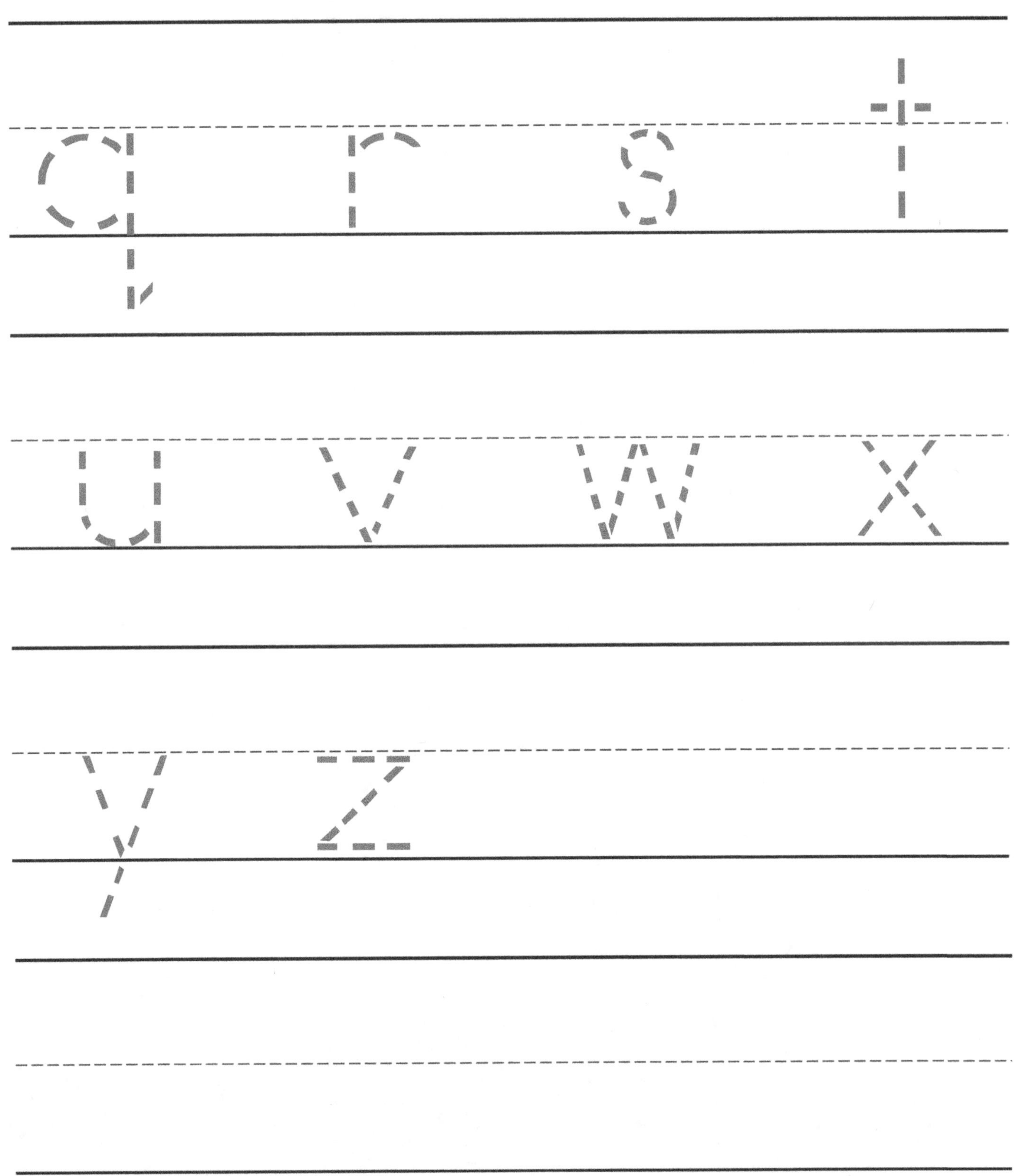

ALPHABET

Trace the small letters.

ALPHABET

Trace the small letters.

PRACTICE!

PRACTICE!

PRACTICE!

PRACTICE!